'S
GUIDE
to
LEGAL
COMPLIANCE

British Retail Consortium
21 Dartmouth Street
London
SW1H 9BP

Telephone: 0207 854 8900
Facimile: 0207 854 8901
Email: info@brc.org.uk
Website: www.brc.org.uk

ISBN 0 11 703199 2
First published 2003

The BRC would like to acknowledge the contribution of Sheila Blowers MATT, Dip2.OSH, MIOSH as author of this work.

Designed and originated by Sarah Haines, TSO
Printed in the United Kingdom by The Stationery Office
N139217 C20   09/03

Contents

1.	**Introduction** – what is this guide for?	**5**
2.	**Management issues**	**7**
	Who is responsible for complying with the law?	7
	Information you must display	8
	Enforcement officers	9
	Compulsory and non-compulsory policies	11
	Carrying out a risk assessment	12
	Safety training	13
	What obligations do you have as an occupier?	14
	What insurance must you have?	15
	What records must you keep?	16
3.	**Trading issues that retailers need to be aware of**	**17**
	What do Trading Standards departments do?	17
	Sale of goods and services	18
	What protection do consumers have?	20
	Age-restricted sales products	21
	Data protection	23
	Sunday trading	24
	Food hygiene and safety	25
4.	**Staff working environment**	**27**
	Have you ensured the health, safety and welfare of your staff?	27
	Violence and aggression against staff	29
	Stress in the workplace	30
5.	**Employees' rights**	**31**
	Equal opportunities	32
	Pay and conditions	33
	Communication between staff and employer	36
	Disability discrimination	37
	Young people	38
6.	**Working safely in the workplace**	**39**
	Work equipment	39
	Manual handling	40
	Lifting operations	41

Maintenance management of work equipment 41
Personal protective equipment 42
Safety signs 43
Safe access 44
New and expectant mothers 46
Workstation safety 47
Working outdoors 48
Staff who have to work on their own 49
Water safety 50

7. Accidents 51
Preventing accidents 51
What should you do if an accident has occurred on your premises? 52

8. Fire 53
Fire protection and prevention: what should you do? 53
Fire-fighting equipment 55

9. Workplace hazards 57
Noise in the workplace 57
Slips, trips and falls 58
Electricity 59
Hand–arm vibration 60
Chemical hazards 61
Hazardous substances 62
Asbestos 63
Vehicles 64

10. Environmental issues 65

11. Legislation 67

12. Useful sources of information 69

1 Introduction – what is this guide for?

There are many areas of legislation affecting retailers and retail activities, and their requirements can change frequently. The purpose of this guide is to outline these legal requirements and to provide you with basic awareness of the issues you need to deal with. Tips are provided on health and safety, environmental and employment issues, and a few more general topics.

If things do go wrong, finding yourself on the wrong side of legislation could be financially crippling, would certainly be time-consuming and make 'business as usual' very difficult. This Guide aims to give you straightforward information about the steps that you should take to begin to comply with the regulations.

The information given in this guide takes the form of key guidance points, supplemented by suggestions for further sources of specialist help if you need it. Many sources are website addresses but if you do not have access to the internet you should be able to get the information from your local library, local authority or trade association.

Please bear in mind that, in health and safety matters, the law assumes a business to be 'guilty until proven innocent', and it is for a business to prove that it has complied with the law. It is, therefore, in your best interests to be able to demonstrate that you operate the correct procedures.

NB The guidance in this booklet is based on English law. If your premises are in Scotland, Wales or Northern Ireland, you should check with your local authority or trade association whether there are any different or additional requirements you need to comply with.

2 Management issues

Who is responsible for complying with the law?

The person who is deemed to be 'in charge' of the business bears the ultimate responsibility for ensuring the compliance of that business with all relevant legal requirements, even if an act or omission that causes a breach of those requirements is carried out by someone else.

Such responsibilities range from legislation that you must comply with, such as the Health and Safety Act, and Occupier's Liability Acts 1957 and 1984, to liaising and co-operating with officers from the Health and Safety Executive (HSE) or Environmental Health or Trading Standards departments. Therefore it is important that you know your responsibilities and keep appropriate records *(see page 16)* as evidence that you are complying with them.

Appoint a competent deputy to take charge at any time when you are absent from the premises. You should also ensure that all members of your staff know that they are accountable for their own and their colleagues' health and safety while at work.

Information you must display

There are certain posters and notices that you must display for the information of your employees, which are described below.

'Health and Safety Law – What You Need to Know' poster

This gives your staff information on the law as it applies to them while they are at work and tells them whom to contact if they have any queries or complaints.

Employers' Liability certificate

This shows your staff that you have insurance to cover any claims arising from accidents at work (see page 15).

Fire action notices

These give details of the action to take on discovering a fire, and where to assemble outside the building. You need to ensure that everyone is familiar with the escape routes from the premises and knows where to assemble so that you can check that each person is accounted for when there is an emergency (see page 53).

First-aider lists

You should list the names of your first-aiders on appropriately placed notices so that all staff can see who is qualified to help them if they are injured or fall ill at work.

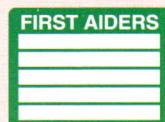

Emergency Plan

You may find it useful to list the appropriate procedures that staff must follow in case of the following emergencies: fires; natural disasters; bomb scares; accidents; violence at work.

Enforcement officers

Retail premises normally come under local authority environmental health officer (EHO) control but, exceptionally, HSE enforcement officers may visit. You should make sure that you know the address and contact number of your local enforcement officer.

Trading standards officers can also visit to check that you comply with regulations relating to the sale of goods.

Why do they visit?
Enforcement officers may visit your premises for a variety of reasons, for instance:

- *in response to a reported accident or incident under the Reporting of Injuries, Diseases and Dangerous Occurrences Regulations 1995 (RIDDOR)*
- *in response to a complaint from a member of the public (enforcement officers have to investigate any complaint made in connection with a business)*
- *when you are due for a routine visit*
- *to check whether new legislation is understood and being implemented*
- *to check on the possible sale of prohibited or faulty goods*
- *to ensure current health and safety, and employment legislation is being observed*
- *to check age-related issues, such as sales and employment.*

What powers and authority do enforcement officers possess?
Enforcement officers are legally entitled to enter your premises for the purpose of helping you to comply with the law. If you resist their entry, they can enlist the help of the police to enforce the law.

What do they look for or ask to see?
This will depend on the reason for their visit. However, they will invariably ask to see:

- *your safety policy (applicable if there are five or more employees)*
- *written risk assessments, which will be asked for whatever the purpose of the visit but especially if there has been an accident*
- *training records for staff – even during a routine visit*
- *compliance with legal requirements; these requirements will be peculiar to the business being carried out.*

What happens if I fail to comply with what an EHO requires?

In some cases EHOs may find it necessary to issue improvement and/or prohibition notices.

Improvement notices give notification of the need for improvement in a situation that has been identified as being in breach of legislation. You are given a realistic timescale in which to take necessary action to bring you into compliance.

Prohibition notices are issued immediately if a situation is perceived as being too dangerous for work to continue. For instance, a food store infested with vermin would be forced to close straightaway and would not be allowed to reopen until the enforcement officer had visited again to check on the remedial action taken.

Both types of notice are followed up by the issuing officers and may be removed only by these officers, when they are content that you have remedied the situation satisfactorily.

Legal implications

There are heavy penalties for ignoring notices and it is a criminal offence to continue trading if a prohibition notice has been served on your business. In extreme circumstances you may face prosecution that results in a fine or even imprisonment.

Appealing against an officer's request

There are formal procedures for appealing against an officer's request. If you consider that a notice has been issued unfairly, you may appeal against it within 21 days of issue, stating clearly the reasons for your appeal. However, generally, you must carry out the demands while an appeal is pending.

Can I ask for advice?

Enforcement officers are required to provide information, advice and support relating to matters within their spheres of responsibility.

What if I'm not available when an enforcement officer visits?

If possible, you should nominate a member of staff who has good knowledge of your business to be there in your absence. The staff member should know where to find all relevant information and be able to answer the enforcement officer's questions satisfactorily.

Compulsory and non-compulsory policies

Some policies are obligatory and these are discussed below.

Health and safety policy

If you employ five or more people, there is a legal requirement for you to have a policy document undertaking to provide healthy and safe working conditions for all your staff. You need to state:

- *how you manage health and safety*
- *who does what*
- *when and how they do it.*

The policy statement should be succinct, with information on individual aspects of health and safety, such as:

- *risk assessment (see page 12)*
- *work equipment (see page 39)*
- *accident reporting (see page 52).*

You can get more information from the HSE booklet *'Stating Your Business',* IND(G)324.

Consumer rights

Your customers have rights under various items of legislation to expect certain standards relating to the goods and services you supply *(see page 20)*. It is advisable to display notices telling them of their rights about the sale of goods, returns, exchanges, refunds, etc. Though it is illegal to put up a notice saying 'No Refunds', as this takes away customers' rights *(see page 20)*, retailers do not necessarily have to have a refund policy.

Other policies are non-compulsory but some companies have environmental or quality policies. These are useful for companies to document activities or services so as to show that they are treating specific issues seriously.

Carrying out a risk assessment

Identifying risks

Identifying and controlling risks to the health and safety of your employees, customers or visitors when they are on your premises are key requirements of the Management of Health and Safety at Work Regulations 1999. The concept of risk assessment is straightforward. Ask yourself the following questions in relation to your business:

- *What tasks and activities are involved?*
- *What could go wrong and cause injury or damage?*
- *Who or what could be injured or damaged?*
- *What are you already doing to control the risk?*
- *What else (if anything) do you need to do to reduce the risk even further, or eliminate the risk altogether?*

You need to conduct specific assessments for fire risks *(see page 53)*, hazardous substances *(see page 62)*, new and expectant mothers *(see page 46)*, and young people *(see page 38)*.

Documentation

If you have five or more employees, the results of risk assessments must be documented so that, in the event of an accident occurring and being investigated by an enforcement officer, you have evidence that you assessed the risk and took steps to eliminate it (ideally) or at least to minimise it.*

*If you are still unsure how to go about carrying out a risk assessment seek further advice from sources such as the HSE, your local authority or trade association.

How to carry out a risk assessment

In order to eliminate or reduce risks to a minimum, carry out a risk assessment by following this procedure:

Step 1: Look for the hazards
Step 2: Decide who might be harmed and how
Step 3: Evaluate the risks: are existing precautions adequate or should more be done?
Step 4: Record your findings
Step 5: Review your assessment and revise it if necessary

Visit **www.hse.gov.uk** in order to read their *'Five steps to risk assessment'*.

Safety training

You need to ensure that your staff are not put at risk of injury or ill health because they do not know or fully understand the way to work safely. Staff must be given relevant instruction and training before they are allowed to start work.

Types of training and instruction

Induction training When new staff first arrive, they should be taken round the premises, shown emergency escape exits, toilets, catering facilities, and so on, and told how the business works and what their jobs will entail.

Job-specific training Do not assume that your staff are aware of the procedures necessary to carry out their work safely. Anyone using work equipment of any kind *(see page 39)* must be adequately trained in safe working practice and you must be satisfied that they recognise the risks involved and understand the associated control measures.

Refresher training When staff do the same job for a lengthy period they may develop bad habits or 'shortcuts' that do not comply with best practice. Particularly where their safety is at risk, it is a good idea to issue periodic reminders of the way the job should be done; and it is good practice for employers to carry out spot checks of the job.

Keeping records

You should ensure that staff members sign training forms to prove that they have received safety training for your records.

What obligations do you have as an occupier?

If you occupy premises, as a manager or owner you will have some fundamental obligations under the Occupiers' Liability Acts 1957 and 1984, with which you must comply.

Premises

You have the following obligations concerning premises:

- *If you are the landlord, you are responsible for the maintenance of 'common' areas such as staircases, lobbies and toilets.*
- *If you are not the landlord, you should have a tenancy agreement that tells you who is responsible for maintenance.*
- *In multi-tenancy premises you must share information about any of your activities that might have an impact on your co-tenants – and they must do the same.*

Safety

You have the following obligations concerning safety:

- *You have a duty to see that visitors (both authorised and unauthorised) and other people you share your premises with are not put at risk when on your premises, either as a result of your work activities or because of any unsafe conditions.*
- *Your premises must have safe access (see page 44) for all authorised and unauthorised visitors (i.e. trespassers and burglars).*

Hazards

You have the following obligations concerning hazards:

- *Display appropriate warnings of any hazards that visitors may not be aware of.*

If your visitors include children you must take extra care because they are considered to be less aware of potential dangers than adults are.

What insurance must you have?

Some types of insurance are a legal requirement; whilst other insurance will prudently cover you for claims relating to damage or injury that occurs on your premises or as a result of the goods or services you supply. Such types of insurance include:

- **Employer's liability insurance** Even if you employ only one member of staff you are legally required to take out this insurance against claims made relating to injury or damage sustained while at work.

- **Public liability insurance** As well as being insured for injuries to staff, you are legally required also to be covered against accidents to people visiting your premises.

- **Product liability insurance** This covers you for any claims made by your customers if you supply defective products. In some cases the fault may not actually be yours but may be traceable back to the manufacturer. In such circumstances you may have to honour claims in the first instance but may then be able to reclaim the expense from the manufacturer.

- **Professional indemnity insurance** If you provide services, as opposed to goods, you may be subject to complaints from customers about the service that they received. This insurance provides protection against such situations and you should consider taking out cover, especially if the service you provide is consultancy. Note that most professional bodies have professional indemnity cover and in some cases, it is compulsory to have this.

Other types of insurance that you might need – depending on the nature of your business – include: property and buildings, business assets and equipment, business interruption, key man cover, goods in transit and health insurance for employees. You can get details from various sources, including your trade association or *www.startinbusiness.co.uk*.

What records must you keep?

It is very important to keep records to show that you are complying with legal requirements and best practice.

You should maintain test and inspection records for:

- *fire alarm tests*
- *emergency lighting*
- *fire extinguishers, hose reels and dry risers*
- *smoke and heat detectors*
- *portable electrical appliances (electrical integrity and microwave leak tests)*
- *machinery and equipment maintenance*
- *personal protective equipment*
- *calibration of weighing and measuring equipment.*

You should also record details of:

- *emergency evacuations*
- *environmental issues (such as emissions and waste disposal)*
- *training (such as induction, job-specific or safety)*
- *risk assessments*
- *remedial action taken relating to improvement or prohibition notices.*

3 Trading issues that retailers need to be aware of

What do Trading Standards departments do?

Trading Standards departments have responsibility for enforcing a wide range of consumer law, including fair trading, consumer protection and environmental safety.

Does your business require a special licence?

General aspects of trading standards are covered in this guide but you should find out whether there is any specific legislation that applies to your particular business. There are special licences for different types of goods, such as food, alcohol or tobacco products, pets, or if you provide services involving skin piercing (tattooing or acupuncture). Alternatively, if your business lends money, offers or arranges credit, leases or rents out goods, you need a credit licence. These licences are issued by the Consumer Credit Licensing Bureau at the Office of Fair Trading.

Check whether any licensing applies to you before commencing trading.

Complaints

Please bear in mind that customers who have been sold unsafe goods can complain to the Trading Standards department and the vendor(s) involved can be heavily fined or even imprisoned for failing to meet safety regulations.

Advice

You can get advice on these and other issues from your local Trading Standards department or from websites such as *www.tradingstandards.gov.uk*, *www.businesslink.org* or *www.bcentral.co.uk*

Sale of goods and services

The law relating to the sale of goods and services covers a wide range of issues, such as the provision and description of goods and services, safety of goods for sale, pricing, labelling, and weights and measures. These requirements are only described briefly here and it is in your best interests to find out exactly how each part of the law relates to your business.

Provision

The following rules apply:

- *The law requires you to ensure that the goods you sell are of satisfactory quality.*
- *Goods you sell must be fit for the purpose for which they were intended, satisfactory in appearance and finish, free from defects, safe and durable, and as described.*
- *Goods sold for use at work must be accompanied by adequate instructions, and material safety data sheets must be supplied with hazardous substances (see also page 61).*
- *Services must be provided with reasonable care and skill, within a reasonable time, and for a reasonable charge.*

The Trade Descriptions Act 1968

The following rules apply:

- *Descriptions of goods and services must be accurate, honest, clear, up to date and exactly as suppliers describe them.*
- *The Trade Descriptions Act makes it illegal to give false descriptions of goods, to supply mis-described goods or to make false statements about services offered.*

Safety

The following general rules apply:

- *The goods you supply must be as safe as reasonably practicable.*
- *Always buy from reputable suppliers.*
- *Check products for damage or obvious safety problems before you put them out for sale.*

There are specific safety requirements for many types of goods (for instance, toys, furnishings and electrical items) and you should make sure that you comply with these if they are applicable.

Pricing

The following rules apply:

- *Prices on or near goods for sale must be unambiguous, clearly legible, easily identifiable with the items to which they refer, and they must have VAT included where relevant.*
- *Price reductions and special offers must be clearly explained.*
- *The unit price of goods – that is, the final price including VAT and taxes for one individual item – sold by quantity or weight must be shown, as required by the Price Marking Order 1999. This does not apply to shops smaller than 280 square metres (3,000 square feet).*
- *Price comparisons must be factual, clearly explained, not misleading and valid.*

Labelling

The following rules apply:

- *Second-hand goods, those with slight defects, or those that are shop-soiled must be clearly labelled as such, in order not to mislead customers into thinking that they are being offered new or 'perfect' items.*
- *If labelling food (see also page 25), ingredients must be clearly stated in order to minimise the risk of harm to allergy sufferers and to draw the attention of vegetarians or vegans to the presence of any animal derivatives.*
- *Any food products that you buy should already be suitably labelled but if you make food on your premises you must ensure that you label it correctly before displaying it for sale.*

Weights and measures

The following rules apply:

- *You must display weights in metric units for all goods you sell loose or prepacked.*
- *Imperial measures may also be shown but they must not be as prominent as the metric ones.*
- *If you supply loose goods, weigh them in view of the customer, using legally approved and accurately calibrated weighing and measuring equipment.*
- *It is illegal to give short weight or measure.*

What protection do consumers have?

Legislation
The most important legislation that protects consumer rights is the Consumer Protection Act 1987. Other relevant legislation includes the Fair Trading Act 1973, the Consumer Credit Act 1974, the Sale of Goods Act 1979, the Food Safety Act 1990, the Consumer Protection (Distance Selling) Regulations 2000 and the Sale and Supply of Goods to Consumers Regulations 2002.

Your local Trading Standards office or relevant trade association can give you detailed information and advice on what you need to do to comply with consumer legislation.

Refunds
If any goods – or services – do not meet any one of the rules for the sale of goods and services shown under 'Provision' on *page 18,* the customer may be entitled to a refund. An offer of a credit note instead does not have to be accepted but, if it is, a refund cannot be claimed later. The customer may be prepared to accept a repair or replacement but if such an offer is unsatisfactory to them you must offer a refund.

Customers are entitled to their money being refunded if the goods or services they have purchased are not of satisfactory quality. Grievances should be raised within a 'reasonable time', but 'reasonable' is not precisely defined. This entitlement applies equally to goods purchased at the full price and those bought in a sale.

Proof of purchase
Proof of purchase can be an invoice, cheque stub or credit card receipt, all of which may be accepted as evidence of purchase.

By law, the only person who can return an item and ask for a refund is the purchaser. However, if someone returns something that was given as a gift, most retailers are willing to waive the requirement to see a receipt.

Non-refundable items
There are some circumstances in which you are not required to give a refund. These include where the customer has changed his or her mind about wanting the goods, where a fault was pointed out at the time of sale and the customer accepted it, or when damage has been caused by the customer after purchase.

Age-restricted sales products

There are products that, by law, you must not supply to people under a specified age and doing so could lead to prosecution. In some cases it is important to know whether a product is being bought for the purpose for which it is intended. All staff should know what the common age-related restrictions on sales are. They are described below.

Common age-related restrictions on sales

If you sell tobacco products over the counter you must display a notice stating that: 'It is illegal to sell tobacco products to persons under 16 years of age.'

If you sell tobacco products from vending machines, the area where the machines are located must be supervised and you must display a notice stating that: 'This machine is only for the use of people aged 16 and over.'

If you sell alcohol you must display a notice that states: 'You must be at least 18 years or over to buy alcohol. It is an offence for those of 18 years or over to buy alcohol on behalf of or for consumption by persons under 18.'

If you sell lottery tickets you must display a sign stating that it is illegal for people under 16 years of age to buy them.

If you sell fireworks (including sparklers) you must be sure that your customers are over 18 years old (16 years old in the case of party poppers and other novelty items).

If you sell solvent-based substances you may do so to people under 18 years old if you believe that they are being bought for the purpose for which they are intended, e.g. nail polish remover. If you believe that they are being requested for inhalation or intoxication, you must refuse sales to people under this age.

If you sell gas lighter refills you must be sure that your customers are over 18 years old.

If you sell or rent videos, DVDs or computer games you must not do so to people who are – or appear to be and cannot prove otherwise – under the age shown on the case and product.

If you sell knives or other bladed items you must not do so to anyone under 16 years old.

If you sell chocolate liqueurs you must not do so to anyone under 16 years of age.

What to do if you or your staff are in doubt about the age of a customer

As an employer, you must put in place and implement a straightforward procedure for dealing with occasions when you have doubts about the age of a customer. If necessary, staff should refuse to serve customers whom they consider under age.

For further information refer to the British Retail Consortium booklet *'Age Restricted Sales'* (available from TSO, *www.tso.co.uk*). The Trading Standards Service Authority also provides information *(www.tradingstandards.gov.uk)*.

Data protection

Whatever your business, you are likely to hold information about your customers in some form or other and, therefore, are required to comply with the provisions of the Data Protection Act 1998.

Principles of good practice for businesses that process (hold) personal data
There are eight principles of good practice for any business that processes personal data. The data must:

- *be fairly and lawfully obtained/recorded*
- *be processed for limited purposes*
- *be adequate, relevant and not excessive*
- *be accurate*
- *not be kept any longer than necessary*
- *be processed in accordance with the data subject's rights (this means that people are entitled to be informed about all the information held about them, to have inaccurate data removed or corrected, and to claim compensation if the information is used in contravention of the Act)*
- *be secure*
- *not be transferred to countries without adequate protection.*

The Information Commissioner

The Information Commissioner is an independent supervisory authority that enforces the Data Protection Act 1998.

If the only data you have relates to staff administration, marketing, advertising, accounting and record keeping (customer names, addresses, credit card details, and so on), you may be exempt from having to contact the Information Commissioner. There is a self-assessment guide for exemptions from the Information Commissioner's Office (*www.dataprotection.gov.uk*; information line 01625 545745; notification helpline 01625 545740).

CCTV

If your premises are protected by closed circuit television you must display a notice to this effect, so that anyone entering is made aware that their presence will be recorded on film.

Sunday trading

The Sunday Trading Act 1994 sets out specific conditions for retail trading on Sundays.

Conditions for retail trading on Sundays

- *If your shop trading area covers less than 280 square metres (3,000 square feet) there are no restrictions on opening hours, so you may open all day on Sundays if you wish to do so. You do not need to notify your local authority of your opening hours.*
- *If your shop trading area covers more than 280 square metres (3,000 square feet) you may still open on Sundays but only for six hours between 10am and 6pm. However, you may not open on Easter Sunday or on Christmas Day when it falls on a Sunday. You must inform your local authority, in writing, of your intention to open on Sundays – 14 days before you do so – because the authority has to maintain a register of premises that operate Sunday trading.*

There are exceptions for particular trades such as farm shops, shops selling alcohol, and motor/cycle accessory shops, which can open all hours regardless of size.

In general, there are no restrictions on the type of goods you can sell on Sundays but there are some restrictions on particular products, e.g. alcohol. Employers who trade on Sundays must also note that there may be restrictions on loading and unloading at large shops on Sundays. Check before you begin trading.

Do your staff want to work on Sundays or not?
By law, staff cannot be forced to work on Sundays if they do not wish to for whatever reason, nor must they be dismissed or penalised for this *(see also page 35)*. However, any staff whose terms and conditions of employment include a contractual requirement to work regular or occasional Sundays are expected to comply with it.

Food hygiene and safety

Legislation

You must comply with the requirements of the Food Safety Act 1990 relating to safety, labelling *(see page 19)*, composition, use of additives and chemicals, specific foodstuffs, and weights and measures *(see page 19)*. Get further information from the Food Standards Agency at *www.foodstandards.gov.uk*.

Non-compliance with food hygiene and safety legislation
There are four broad categories of offence for non-compliance with food hygiene and safety legislation:

- *rendering food injurious to health*
- *selling or having food for sale that does not meet food safety requirements (such as food past its use-by date)*
- *selling food that is not of the quality demanded by the purchaser*
- *falsely describing, advertising or presenting food.*

Enforcement

Environmental health officers, trading standards officers, local authorities and the Food Standards Agency (FSA) enforce food law. In order to ensure that you do comply, pay attention to storage, handling and cleanliness.

Hazard Analysis Critical Control Points (HACCP)

HACCP is a food safety management system that is effective in ensuring food hygiene and safety is carried out to the highest standards. Training is available from the BRC.

Storage and handling

Advice about storage and handling:

- *Keep chilled and frozen food in refrigerated storage at the correct temperature. Don't allow frozen food to thaw and then refreeze it.*
- *Segregate raw and cooked foodstuffs, particularly meats.*
- *Check that packaging is intact. Remove any items where the wrapping is damaged, as the food could have become contaminated.*
- *Check 'sell-by' dates regularly – don't leave outdated food on general display. You may still sell items that have reached their 'best before' date.*
- *Don't let people handle food if they have skin infections, infected wounds, or diarrhoea.*
- *If you are serving hot food to customers, make sure that it is heated right through.*
- *Do not allow food waste or other refuse to accumulate anywhere, and especially not in areas where food is prepared.*

Cleanliness

Advice about cleanliness:

- *Keep your premises clean – this includes walls, floors, paintwork and all surfaces where food is prepared.*
- *Wash hands thoroughly before and after handling food, after using the toilet, and between handling food and money.*
- *Ensure that clothing worn by food handlers is kept clean – or changed promptly if it gets messy.*
- *Provide protective clothing such as aprons and overalls, and ensure that these are cleaned or replaced regularly.*
- *Arrange for your staff to be provided with training in food hygiene, and encourage them to operate to best practice at all times.*
- *Where food is being manufactured, prepared or served, no smoking is allowed.*

Remember: food hygiene and safety should be practical; safety checks should be regularly carried out, understood by staff, and records should be kept.

4 Staff working environment

Have you ensured the health, safety and welfare of your staff?

Working conditions for staff
Under the Workplace (Health, Safety and Welfare) Regulations 1992 it is the employer's responsibility to make proper arrangements in the following areas:

Ventilation
There must be a source of fresh air, either by natural ventilation (doors and windows), or by mechanical extraction or forced ventilation systems. Enclosed spaces must be adequately ventilated.

Temperature
The recommended minimum indoor temperature is 16°C or 13°C where the work involves heavy lifting or manual activities.

Lighting
There must be sufficient lighting to enable people to carry out their work in safety and without undue strain on their eyes. Stairs and corridors must be well lit.

Noise
Your staff may be subject to intrusive background noise from machinery or equipment being used for the job, or noise from other operations nearby. If excessive, you should arrange for a noise survey to be carried out *(see also page 57)*.

Sanitary facilities
These must be provided on the premises and should ideally comprise separate toilets for men and women, and washing facilities. You may also need to provide facilities for staff with physical disabilities and for customers *(see also page 37)* if your business is one where food may be eaten on the premises.

Rest room facilities
You must provide somewhere where your staff can take their rest breaks away from the workplace, and include suitable seating, especially if staff have to stand for long periods while they are at work.

Facilities for clothing

Staff should have somewhere to store their outdoor clothing, bags and other items while they are at work; when staff have to change into different clothes for work, lockers should be provided.

Catering facilities

Provide the means for your staff to make hot drinks and, ideally, to prepare food for themselves. In small premises, this may well be just a kettle and perhaps a microwave oven for heating food. Any such items must be tested regularly for electrical integrity *(see page 59)*, to ensure that they are safe for use.

Drinking water

There must be a source of clean drinking water on the premises – a tap clearly marked 'drinking water', bottled water or a water cooler.

Cleanliness and waste

You should make sure that the premises are kept as clean and tidy as possible, avoiding any build-up of waste materials or debris that could pose a slipping or tripping hazard *(see page 58)* or be unhygienic, especially where food is handled *(see page 26)*.

Violence and aggression against staff

You are required by law to provide your staff with a healthy and safe working environment. Violence and aggression may be encountered in any workplace as a result of accessibility to members of the public, having money on the premises or in transit to the bank, from road rage, or as a result of stressful work situations.

What can help eliminate or reduce the risk of violence?
Identify the types of violence and the areas where violence and aggression might be encountered in your business with a risk assessment *(see page 12)*, then implement appropriate measures to eliminate or reduce those risks. Controls might include panic buttons, screens to separate staff from customers, personal alarms; or changing the job design, for instance encouraging cashless transactions, varying banking routines, avoiding situations where staff work alone *(see page 49)*.

You should:

- *ask staff whether they have any problems*
- *involve staff in developing controls or changing procedures, as this should help to ensure that they are implemented*
- *give staff support, the opportunity to talk about their anxieties and experiences, and time off if they need it after an incident.*

Dealing with potentially aggressive people
Advise staff to handle a potentially explosive situation in the following way:

- *Remain calm, be polite, do not raise your voice.*
- *Call for assistance from colleagues, or the police if necessary.*
- *Keep out of reach of the aggressor.*
- *Do not antagonise, abuse or ridicule the aggressor.*
- *Do not try and detain the aggressor.*

Report incidents involving violence and aggression to the Health and Safety Executive or your local authority under the Reporting of Injuries, Diseases and Dangerous Occurrences Regulations 1995 (RIDDOR). It may also be necessary to involve the police.

Stress in the workplace

Causes of stress and its effects
Stress can be caused by harassment or bullying, personality clashes, heavy workload or lack of work, lack of management support, disillusionment, low morale and external pressures. The effects of workplace stress on a business can include increased levels of ill health, sickness absence, poor timekeeping, reduced timekeeping and customer complaints.

Employer and employee awareness
Employers have been successfully prosecuted for allowing situations to develop (or continue) that are detrimental to the physical and/or mental well-being of their staff. As an employer, it is advisable to have a public policy for dealing with stress.

Employees should be made aware that there is a health and safety duty for them to inform their employer of any stressful situations so that the employer can deal with them.

How to deal with staff who suffer from stress
Be prepared to offer sympathy, reassurance and understanding if someone reports the symptoms of stress: try to be flexible in your approach to a solution (which might, for example, involve changing a person's job) and recognise when professional counselling might be appropriate. Above all, you must respect confidentiality.

Finally, do not just address the symptoms of stress – you must try to identify and eliminate (or limit) the hazards causing stress to your employees.

5 Employees' rights

Employment law

Employment law is a vast and complex subject. For information, refer to sources such as:

- *the Advisory, Conciliation and Arbitration Service (ACAS) and 'The A to Z of Work' (www.acas.org.uk), for specific and very helpful advice*
- *Tiger (Tailored Interactive Guidance on Employment Rights) (www.tiger.gov.uk), for general guidance.*

These and other sources will help ensure that you are aware of the employment-related rights that your staff are entitled to.

Equal opportunities

Discrimination
You must not treat any employees or applicants for jobs unfavourably on the grounds of their age, sex, religion, race, colour, sexuality or disability. In addition, where the latter are capable of performing the work involved, you must not discriminate between able-bodied people and those with physical disabilities for employment purposes *(see also page 37)*.

Disciplinary and grievance procedures for employers and employees
When you need to discipline a member of staff for misconduct or failing to meet set working standards, you need to have a procedure in place.

Equally, members of your staff may have some kind of grievance concerning their employment. If such grievances are not addressed they may result in bad employee relations.

Your staff, permanent and temporary, must be provided with information about these procedures so that they know what to expect and do should the need arise.

Part-time staff
Part-time staff are entitled to be treated in the same way as full-time staff. They must receive the same hourly rates of pay and overtime pay, not be excluded from training and have the same entitlements to paid holidays and maternity or paternity leave pro rata to the hours they work as full-time staff.

Staff on short-term contracts
Staff employed for short periods, such as to cover maternity leave or peak periods, should not be treated differently from permanent staff.

Pay and conditions

Are you aware of the pay and working conditions applicable to your staff?

Staff pay
Staff are entitled to be paid at an hourly rate of at least the National Minimum Wage – currently £4.20 per hour, rising to £4.50 per hour in October 2003. Get more information about this from the Department of Trade and Industry (DTI) at *www.dti.gov.uk/er/nmw*. You must also ensure that you pay your staff according to their contracts of employment (see 'Terms and Conditions', below) and that you pay male and female employees the same rate for the same job.

National Insurance contributions must be paid by an employer for any employee over the age of 16 whose earnings exceed the earning threshold – the ACAS booklet 'Introduction to Pay Systems' is one source of information on this. Employees also pay National Insurance contributions.

You must not pay your employees 'out of the till' but must have a pay recording system that allows you to provide them with itemised pay statements so that they can see the gross and net amounts of pay they have received and the deductions that have been made.

Maternity and paternity leave and pay
A pregnant employee can leave work at any time within 11 weeks of the expected date of birth. She is entitled to up to 26 weeks' paid and a further 26 weeks' unpaid leave provided that she has notified you in writing of her pregnancy no later than the end of the 15th week before the week in which the baby is due. New fathers may take up to two weeks' paid leave at the time of the birth. The same amounts of parental leave are allowed in the case of adoption.

Sick pay
If an employee is unable to work for at least 4 days due to illness, as an employer you must pay employees statutory sick pay (SSP) which is the minimum that they should receive in wages. If you pay your staff an occupational sick pay rate – which is their full wage or higher than the SSP rate – then you need not operate the SSP scheme. Refer to the Inland Revenue for full details and any forms that may be required.

Terms and conditions

You are required by law to give a written statement of the main terms and conditions of employment to all your employees within two months of the date they start working for you.

Working hours

The Working Time Regulations 1998, which cover retail staff, were introduced to limit people's working hours to a maximum of 48 hours per week on average, calculated over a rolling 17 week period.

In essence, all staff must have at least 11 hours off in every 24 hour period and at least one day off in any seven day period. An employee voluntarily agreeing to work in excess of the stipulated hours must sign a declaration to this effect and must be made aware that the agreement may be rescinded at any time.

If you employ young people make sure you are familiar with the restrictions on working hours that may be applicable *(see page 38 for further details)*.

Flexible working

Parents of children under 6 years old or parents of children with disabilities under the age of 18 years may ask to work flexible hours to fit in with their children's needs. If any of your staff ask for flexible working hours, you have a statutory duty to consider the request seriously and to give a good reason if you decide not to accommodate it. The key points relating to this procedure are:

- *The employee must apply in writing (and can make only one application per year).*
- *The employer must meet with the employee within 28 days.*
- *The employer must write to the employee within 14 days of the meeting, either stating the new work pattern or giving clear business grounds for refusing the application.*
- *The employee has 14 days to appeal against the decision.*
- *In specific circumstances the claim can be taken to an employment tribunal.*

Holidays

Anyone working full-time is entitled under the provisions of the Working Time Regulations 1998 to a minimum of four weeks' paid holiday per year. You may choose to allow your staff to take public and bank holidays off in addition to the four weeks but you are not legally obliged to do so. If you employ part-time staff you should calculate their holiday entitlement pro rata.

Sunday working

By law, your staff cannot be forced to work on Sundays *(see page 24)* if they do not wish to, and they may not be dismissed or penalised if they state their preference not to work on Sundays. However, any staff whose terms and conditions of employment include a statutory requirement to work regular or occasional Sundays are expected to comply with it.

Training and development

You should provide your staff with appropriate training in order to enable them to do their jobs effectively. They should be given suitable and sufficient instruction on health and safety issues *(see page 13)*, as well as training for the skills they need to do their work. Members of staff may ask you for additional training and you should do your best to arrange this within a reasonable time of the request.

Redundancy

If you have to make employees redundant (for instance, as a result of shop closure or the need to reduce staff numbers), ensure that you behave in accordance with legislative requirements, otherwise you could be sued for unfair dismissal.

Detailed information on all aspects of pay and conditions are available from ACAS (see *'The A to Z of Work'*, *www.acas.org.uk*) or the DTI.

Communication between staff and employer

In order to avoid your staff saying *'I didn't know, nobody told me'*, you are legally obliged to give relevant and up-to-date information on issues that may affect their health and safety, working conditions or employment terms *(see page 34)*. Staff should have the chance to tell you of any queries or concerns they may have on these matters.

You should provide staff with information on:

- **Risks and hazards in the workplace, and the measures in place to control them** *Use the results of your risk assessments (see page 12) for this.*
- **Proposed changes to working procedures** *If staff are invited to contribute to changes they are more likely to accept them; in addition, because they actually do the work, they are likely to have ideas on how things could be improved.*
- **Proposed changes to working conditions** *Ensure that these are in line with employment law.*
- **Action to take if there is an emergency** *Your staff need to know what to do if there is a fire (see page 53) or other emergency situations.*

Methods of communication may involve meetings, handouts, notices, posters and videos. You should also take into account the range of experience, knowledge and training among your staff, as well as any language difficulties or disabilities that might hinder their understanding.

Remember to communicate effectively with any members of staff who work alone *(see page 49)*, or do not work on the premises.

Principles for communicating effectively
In order to communicate effectively with your staff:

- *decide who needs information*
- *decide what information is needed*
- *decide when that information is needed*
- *decide how to provide that information*
- *check that the information has been properly understood and acted upon.*

Disability discrimination

Disability of one kind or another can affect practically anyone in any type of work, and the Disability Discrimination Act 1995 (DDA) makes it unlawful to discriminate against anyone who has a disability. You can find out more information on what you need to do to comply with this legislation from sources such as the Disability Rights Commission, helpline 08457 622633 or website *www.drc-gb.org*, or by searching 'disability' on *www.businesslink.org*.

Are you aware of the different disabilities that staff or customers may have?
People with disabilities may be visually or hearing impaired, have a speech impediment, a learning disability, or a physical disability and possibly be in a wheelchair. Whatever the disability, they must be treated with respect and consideration in accordance with their needs.

DDA and 'service providers'

As of 2004, further legislation will be imposed on retailers and any kind of business that offers access to the public. These 'service providers' will be required to make 'reasonable adjustments' to the physical fabric of their offices/shops. Simple, cost-effective physical changes in the workplace can often be made quite easily or they can be made as part of a planned refurbishment. Consider such actions as:

- *providing automatic sliding doors for easier access*
- *providing wheelchair access, such as ramps*
- *providing hand rails to assist people climbing stairs*
- *leaving as much space as possible between display racks*
- *displaying large-print notices as well as those of standard size*
- *offering help with finding or reaching items, as required*
- *training a few staff to sign for deaf people*
- *providing seats near the till so that people can sit down while they are being served*
- *providing lever taps in washrooms and toilets*
- *providing toilet facilities for staff with physical disabilities, and for customers in places where food may be bought and eaten on the premises*
- *providing car parking and disabled bays – ensuring they are kept free.*

It is important that your staff understand and know how to work with customers and colleagues who have disabilities. They should try to anticipate needs, and be prepared to offer assistance, but should not impose it.

Young people

If you employ young people – those over school leaving age but under 18 years old – they must not work as long hours as adults do and must have longer rest breaks. Refer to the Working Time Regulations 1998 and Working Time (Amendment) Regulations 2002. Note that it is illegal to employ children who are less than 13 years of age.

Young people are not allowed to work on dangerous machinery; they must be supervised by an older person until they are considered competent to do a job on their own; and they must not be left alone on the premises under any circumstances *(see also page 49)*.

When carrying out any risk assessments *(see page 12)* involving young staff you must take into account their inexperience and the fact that they are less likely than older colleagues to be aware of potential hazards.

Summary of the law on employing young people

Children of 13 years and over may work:

- *on schooldays for a maximum of 2 hours*
- *on Saturdays age 13–14, for a maximum of 5 hours; age 15–16, for a maximum of 8 hours*
- *on Sundays for a maximum of 2 hours*
- *during term time for a maximum of 12 hours per week*
- *during school holidays age 13–14, for a maximum of 25 hours per week; age 15–16, for a maximum of 35 hours per week.*

Children must also have a two-week break from any work during the school holidays in each calendar year.

Children may not work:

- *without an employment certificate issued by their local education authority*
- *for more than four hours without a break of at least one hour*
- *for more than one hour before school*
- *during school hours*
- *before 7am or after 7pm*
- *in any industrial setting, for example in a factory*
- *in any occupation prohibited by local bye-laws or other legislation, for instance in pubs, betting shops, or in any other work that may be harmful to their health, well-being or education.*

6 Working safely in the workplace

Work equipment

Do your employees use work equipment?

The term 'work equipment' is taken to be any piece of machinery or equipment provided for use at work. Employers must ensure that such equipment is suitable for its purpose, and that it is safe and well maintained. Complete a risk assessment *(see page 12)* to identify the control measures you need to put in place to protect your staff from harm.

Is the equipment being used properly?

The employees who use the equipment must be suitably trained and competent to do so, and must follow any manufacturers' or suppliers' instructions. No one should be allowed to use equipment without proper training and authorisation.

For further information, refer to the Provision and Use of Work Equipment Regulations 1998 (PUWER) and the Lifting Operations and Lifting Equipment Regulations 1998 (LOLER).

Use guard

Switch off

Manual handling

Many retail jobs involve some element of manual handling but the type of load will vary.

Can the job cause injury?

Incorrect handling techniques are one of the major causes of injury at work, and the effects of bad handling techniques may be cumulative until a relatively simple lifting task results in injury. Very often, injuries are to the lower back, but people may also suffer from strains and sprains.

Employees may also develop symptoms of musculo-skeletal disorders – which are reportable under the Reporting of Injuries, Diseases and Dangerous Occurrences Regulations 1995 (RIDDOR) – or work-related upper limb disorder (WRULD) if jobs involve repetitive lifting, twisting or reaching. (WRULD is another name for repetitive strain injury (RSI).)

How to reduce the risk of injury

Carry out a risk assessment *(see page 12)* to see what additional control measures can reduce the risk of injury to your staff. The elements you should consider are:

- *The task* What activity is involved? How often does it have to be done?
- *The individual* Who does the task? Are individuals of suitable build and strength to manage?
- *The load* What type of loads are involved? Are they large, heavy, unstable, sharp?
- *The environment* Where does the activity take place?

No assumptions should be made regarding individuals and manual handling, risk assessments must be made looking at each case individually. Ideally, find solutions that eliminate the need for manual handling, for instance provide lifting aids such as trolleys or hoists *(see page 41)*.

Give your staff information on the risks of manual handling and how to control them, for instance by issuing a checklist of tips on good handling techniques or displaying posters.

Lifting operations

Moving goods around your premises

Depending on the size of the items, you might move goods around your premises with a fork-lift truck, hand-operated pallet truck, hoist, trolley or goods lift. If goods are for sale on more than one level you may also have a passenger lift. The Lifting Operations and Lifting Equipment Regulations 1998 (LOLER) require that whatever lifting equipment you use, it must be visually inspected, tested and examined by a competent person:

- *before use for the first time*
- *following modification or repair*
- *at intervals in accordance with legislation.*

In addition, the safe working load must be displayed and must not be exceeded. Anyone who operates lifting equipment must be fully trained and competent to do the job. You should also ensure that refresher training *(see page 13)* is given at regular intervals.

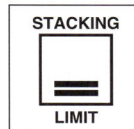

Maintenance management of work equipment

If you rely on machinery and equipment to carry out your business, you should ensure that everything is regularly maintained and that the equipment is safe to use. Under the Provision and Use of Work Equipment Regulations 1998 (PUWER) you should put in place maintenance schedules for the items used in your business activities.

Maintenance schedules

These are legislative requirements relating to the frequency and thoroughness of tests and inspections, particularly for those items of powered machinery and equipment with the potential to cause injury or damage if they don't work properly. You should keep records of all inspections and maintenance work that has been carried out *(see page 16)* as these will be required in the event of an accident investigation or if you need to claim for compensation from the supplier if the equipment fails or causes damage to other property.

Personal protective equipment

Do staff require protection against hazards in their job?

The nature of an employee's job might require them to use personal protective equipment (PPE), which might include any of the following: gloves or gauntlets, eye protection, hearing protection, safety footwear, aprons or overalls. The type of protection required will depend on the nature of the hazard. If PPE is necessary, you must provide it at no cost to the employees involved.

Assess the range of PPE available, as it is important to ensure that you select the right type for the purpose – for instance, if eye protection is required, you need to consider whether goggles, glasses or a visor would be most appropriate.

You need to make sure that staff who are issued with PPE know:

- *why it is being issued (important if you want to ensure it is worn)*
- *how and when it is to be used*
- *how to look after it*
- *what to do if it needs repair or replacement.*

If PPE is specific to one area of your premises only, it is a good idea to put up notices or signs *(see page 43)* as reminders to staff to use it in that area. Make sure that employees know that it is a disciplinary offence to refuse to wear PPE that has been identified as necessary for them to carry out their job, and be specific about what sort of equipment this is.

| *Ear protection* | *Eye protection* | *Hand protection* | *Protective clothing* | *Protective footwear* |

Safety signs

What are safety signs and when should they be used?

Safety signs are used to convey a wide range of information, and provide messages that can be easily understood. You have a legal obligation to provide safety signs wherever there is a risk that you have not been able to communicate fully by other means. You must obtain and display appropriate safety signs where there is a risk to the health and safety of your staff and/or your customers.

Signs incorporate certain colours, shapes and symbols (pictograms) to indicate specific hazards or instructions:

- **Prohibition signs** indicate danger, e.g. 'No access to unauthorised personnel'.

- **Warning signs** indicate 'be careful', e.g. 'Take care, slippery floor', 'Danger, high voltage'.

- **Mandatory signs** give specific instructions, e.g. 'Wear safety shoes' or fire action notices *(see page 53)*.

- **Safe conditions signs** show that something is safe, or indicate the way to safety, e.g. 'First aid room', 'Emergency escape route'.

- **Fire safety signs** are used to indicate the position of fire extinguishers, fire call points, and so on. Fire exits must also be clearly marked, as some of them may be exits other than the normal ones.

You can find out more about safety signs from the Health and Safety (Safety Signs and Signals) Regulations 1996.

Safe access

Providing safe access

You must ensure that your staff, customers and other visitors can access your premises without any undue risk to their safety. As an employer, you should:

- *keep escape routes clear of obstruction*
- *provide hand rails on stairs*
- *ensure that steps and stairs are of equal height*
- *paint warning stripes on the front edge of outside steps and stairs*
- *keep floor surfaces well maintained and repair any faults promptly*
- *put markings onto any glass doors so they are visible.*

Do visitors or customers have access to your business premises?

The Health and Safety at Work Act 1974 imposes legal obligations on employers to introduce sufficient measures and controls to protect members of the public who may have access to their premises, such as visitors, customers and even unauthorised persons.

Are there hazards on the premises?

Where there are known hazards, display adequate and appropriate warning notices, for instance 'Danger', 'Keep Away', 'No Smoking', 'Do Not Touch'. In addition, if it is possible that children could have access to hazards or there is some need for control of the public, you may need to implement additional physical and proactive measures, including 'policing', to ensure that the notices are obeyed.

Are the premises shared with tenants?

If you share your premises with other tenants, each tenant's responsibilities must be clearly understood and there must be communication between tenants, covering topics such as the inspection and maintenance arrangements of access and relevant plant, equipment and fittings.

Any accidents or incidents involving members of the public that occur on your premises must be dealt with in the same way as those involving your staff – they must be recorded in an accident book and may also need to be reported to the HSE *(see page 52)*.

Are contractors employed on the premises?

The Management of Health and Safety at Work Regulations 1999 set out health and safety duties for both clients and contractors.

A permit-to-work system is a formal system that specifies any work that is potentially hazardous – and the precautions to be taken. Work is only begun once safe procedures are defined and a record of all foreseeable hazards has been considered. The HSE provides detailed information about permits-to-work *(www.hse.gov.uk)*.

New and expectant mothers

Is there any part of a pregnant woman's job that could cause a problem during her pregnancy? The same applies to women who come back to work soon after the birth of a baby, or who are breast-feeding.

Workplace activities that might cause new and expectant mothers problems include:
- *working shift patterns or at night*
- *manual handling*
- *working in hot atmospheres*
- *carrying out tasks liable to cause physical or mental fatigue*
- *working on slippery or wet surfaces*
- *carrying out activities where the taking of rest breaks and/or the distance to a rest room or toilet could cause a problem*
- *carrying out work that involves being exposed to hazardous substances.*

If you find that an expectant or new mother could be at risk, you must take suitable steps to minimise (or, ideally, eliminate) the risk. You must also provide suitable rest facilities and encourage expectant and new mothers to take regular breaks.

For further information, the Management of Health and Safety at Work Regulations 1999 includes regulations to protect new and expectant mothers; refer to *'The A to Z of Work'* by ACAS *(www.acas.org.uk)*; and the HSE provides health and safety information *(www.hse.gov.uk)*.

Workstation safety

The Health and Safety (Display Screen Equipment) Regulations 1992 require you to provide ergonomically sound furniture and surroundings for anyone who uses a visual display unit (VDU) during the working day.

Identify the problem(s)

Identify any issues that may need to be addressed. If staff suffer from aches and pains, it may be due to poor design of the workstations or lack of space around them. If so, then reconsider the design of the workstation and surrounding area. Would a different chair or footrest make a difference? If the issues are more problematic, you may need to engage the help of someone qualified in ergonomics.

Do your staff use computers or visual display units?

Staff should be made aware of the symptoms of repetitive strain injury (RSI)/ work-related upper limb disorder (WRULD) and report them should they develop.

If employees use VDUs for a large part of day, they are entitled to have eye tests paid for by you as their employer. If staff need spectacles especially for VDU work, you are required by law to pay for them, or provide a contribution to the cost.

VDU operators should also be provided with adequate and appropriate training in the software that they are expected to use, helping to ensure that they do not suffer from any undue stress.

Working outdoors

If your staff work outdoors you must take care that they are suitably protected against the elements.

There is growing awareness of the need to protect against skin cancers: try to ensure that staff keep arms, head, neck and back covered if they are working in the sun. You may need to provide protection such as hats, loose shirts or supplies of sun-block cream.

On the other hand, if you have people who work outdoors in cold conditions – or in refrigerated areas – you should provide them with suitable hats, coats, gloves and boots so that they are not adversely affected by the cold.

Exposure times should also be controlled. Staff should not work in any extremes of temperature for prolonged periods; make sure that they have the opportunity to take regular breaks to go indoors/move to somewhere at normal room temperature and take refreshment.

Staff who have to work on their own

Are there situations when staff have to work alone on the premises? You need to be aware of potential risks and take suitable action to control them.

Identify the tasks, hazards, existing controls and whether any additional measures are necessary with a risk assessment (see also page 12).

Risk assessment for staff working alone
The questions you might ask in a risk assessment include:

- *What is the task? Does it involve anything hazardous, which should not be undertaken without someone else present in case of accident?*
- *Is the lone worker suitable for the task? The consideration is whether the worker is, for instance, pregnant, has any physical disability, inexperienced, or physically unfit. Anyone left alone on the premises should be mature, sensible, responsible and physically capable.*
- *Is there a risk of violence to the lone worker?*
- *Is there some way for the lone worker to raise an alarm if necessary – and do they know what it is?*
- *Does the lone worker know what to do if there is an emergency? For instance, does the worker know the way out of the building if the normal exits are closed, and the number to call to raise an alarm?*

Employers must comply with the Health and Safety at Work Act 1974, and the Management of Health and Safety at Work Regulations 1999. Consult the HSE (*www.hse.gov.uk*) for further information on lone workers.

Water safety

Have you ensured that the water on your premises is safe?
Legislation such as The Health and Safety at Work Act 1974 and the Control of Substances Hazardous to Health Regulations 1988 requires employers to ensure that water used on their premises is safe. It is your legal duty to prevent and control the risk of legionnaires' disease in the water system.

There is an approved code of practice that explains what employers should do. The HSE can provide further information *(www.hse.gov.uk)*.

Precautionary measures if you work with water
Where your business involves water, for instance if you display water features at a garden centre, the measures you might put in place include:

- *regular inspection of your water system by experts*
- *erecting barriers to prevent people – especially children – falling into the water (or interfering with the feature)*
- *displaying appropriate warning and safety signs (see page 43)*
- *ensuring that the water temperature is maintained at a level that is not conducive to the growth of legionella bacteria (see above)*
- *switching water features on for at least part of the day, to ensure that water is not allowed to stagnate in the piping, as this is an environment in which legionella bacteria can breed.*

7 Accidents

Preventing accidents

Wherever possible use precautionary measures in order to prevent accidents taking place. This should help reduce the number of accidents and the need for first aid. If an accident happens, first aid can be used to treat minor injuries; if there is a serious accident call for emergency help immediately. Only people trained to use first aid should treat the patient in these circumstances. The HSE (*www.hse.gov.uk*) provides basic first aid advice, including a FAQ sheet about first aid at work.

First aid

You have a legal obligation to provide properly equipped first aid boxes on your premises for use in the event of accidents. If you buy ready-filled boxes they contain only the items that first-aiders at work are allowed to use, together with a list of those items that you can refer to when you need to restock.

Small premises may well not have a fully qualified first-aider but the Health and Safety (First Aid) Regulations 1981 require that there should be an 'appointed person' who looks after the first aid arrangements and can take charge if there is an accident or someone falls ill at work. One-day courses are available; contact your local St John Ambulance or British Red Cross.

Do you have qualified first-aiders?

Anyone who qualifies as an appointed person or first-aider should be covered by your company's Employers' Liability insurance *(see page 15)* for aid they give on the premises. They may also subscribe to their own insurance through the professional organisation they qualify with, which gives added security if they are involved in any incidents outside the working environment.

In an emergency:
- *assess the situation*
- *make the area safe*
- *assess all casualties and attend those unconscious first*
- *do not delay in sending for help*
- *follow the ABC of resuscitation (Airway, Breathing, Circulation).*

What should you do if an accident has occurred on your premises?

Accident book
You must keep an accident book on your premises and all accidents – whether to staff or the public – must be reported, however trivial they may appear at the time. Also record 'near-miss' incidents – events that did not result in injury but which might do if they happened again.

Accidents may result in damage to property as well as injury to people, and these should also be recorded, especially if you are likely to need details for an insurance claim.

TSO has launched a new Accident Book which will help employers comply with Data Protection regulations, and will be enforceable from 31 December 2003.

Investigate and implement
Recording incidents helps to identify trends; for instance repeated accidents involving the same equipment, activity or member of staff would indicate the need to investigate the equipment or activity and implement any remedial action as necessary.

Was more than basic first aid required?
If someone has an accident on your premises that involves the need for more than basic first aid, you must investigate the cause of the accident, identify any controls that might be required to stop similar accidents happening in future, and implement those controls.

RIDDOR and form F2508
In compliance with the Reporting of Injuries, Diseases and Dangerous Occurrences Regulations 1995 (RIDDOR), any accident resulting in a member of the public being removed from the premises by ambulance or an employee being off sick for more than three working days must be reported to the HSE using form F2508. Books of these forms are available from the HSE (0845 300 9923) or you can complete entries electronically on the HSE website *www.hse.gov.uk*.

8 Fire

Fire protection and prevention: what should you do?

Fire safety education is focused around prevention, detection and escape.

Are fire risks properly controlled?

You are required by law to ensure that workplace fire risks are properly controlled. Under the Fire Precautions (Workplace) Regulations 1997 (as amended 1999) you must:

- *carry out and document a fire risk assessment (see below)*
- *have suitable fire detection and warning arrangements*
- *make sure that people can get out of the building safely*
- *provide, check and maintain suitable fire fighting equipment (see page 55)*
- *make sure that your staff know what to do in the event of fire.*

Fire risk assessments

When carrying out a fire risk assessment you should ask the following questions:

- *What combustible materials are there on the premises (e.g. paper, card, textiles, aerosols)?*
- *What sources of ignition are there (e.g. cooking appliances, smokers' materials, naked flames)?*
- *Who could be hurt if there is a fire?*
- *What systems are there to detect and give warning of fires (e.g. smoke detectors, heat detectors, fire alarms)?*
- *What do you have to put out fires with (e.g. fire extinguishers, fire blankets, hose reels)?*
- *Are there adequate escape routes leading to a safe assembly area and are they kept clear at all times?*
- *Are escape routes sufficiently well lit (by emergency lighting if the mains power is disconnected) to help people see to get out?*
- *Are staff aware of potential hazards and do they have sufficient information and instruction on what to do and where to assemble if there is a fire?*
- *Are fire action notices and escape route signs clearly displayed?*

Fire alarm tests and fire drills

You must test the fire alarm system once a week and conduct a practice evacuation at least once a year, and record the results *(see page 16)*. If you share your premises with other tenants you should agree when, how and by whom these actions should be carried out.

Fire marshals

If you have a large number of staff or customers, or both, including staff/customers with disabilities, appoint and train some staff as fire marshals, to co-ordinate emergency evacuations.

You can get more advice on fire-related issues from your local fire service; or the Office of the Deputy Prime Minister *(www.odpm.gov.uk)* has information and advice on fire safety and prevention issues.

Fire-fighting equipment

There are a number of different types of fire-fighting equipment including portable fire extinguishers, fire blankets, hose reels and sprinkler systems.

Fire extinguishers

There are different types of fire extinguisher for different types of fire. Be careful to choose the right extinguisher for the type of fire that you might need to put out.

Old style fire extinguishers were identifiable by the colour of the canister but nowadays fire extinguishers are all red (although they may have a panel of the 'old' colour to indicate which type they are).

The following table shows the types of extinguishers, their colours and what kinds of fire they should (and should not) be used for:

Type	Colour	Use(s)
Water	Red	Organic materials such as wood, paper, textiles. Not to be used on electrical, cooking oil or fat fires.
Foam	Red with a cream panel	Organic materials such as wood, paper, textiles; flammable liquids. Not to be used on electrical, cooking oil or fat fires.
Powder	Red with a blue panel	Organic materials such as wood, paper, textiles; flammable liquids, flammable gases. Not to be used on cooking oil or fat fires.
Carbon dioxide	Red with a black panel	Flammable liquids, electrical fires. Not to be used on cooking oil or fat fires.

There is an extinguisher especially for use on cooking oil and fat fires, but this type of appliance should be operated only by people who have been specially trained to use it safely.

Do fire extinguishers require inspection and servicing?

All appliances should be inspected weekly by you or one of your staff, to check for any damage, and must be serviced once a year and the results recorded *(see also page 16)*.

Do staff require training?

If your staff have not been trained in the use of extinguishing equipment, they must not use it. Even if they have been trained, they must only try to tackle a fire if it is safe to do so. The most important thing is to get away from the fire safely.

Contact your local fire service or fire equipment supplier for advice.

9 Workplace hazards

Workplace hazards are numerous. Employers and staff should be as vigilant as possible to prevent accidents or exposure to anything harmful.

Noise in the workplace

Work-induced hearing loss
If staff are frequently exposed to high levels of workplace noise – or to very high levels even for short periods – they may develop symptoms of work-induced hearing loss. The damaging effects may develop gradually but, once present, they are often irreversible.

What must you do if noise levels are unacceptable?
Under the Noise at Work Regulations 1989, if statutory limits are exceeded employers must reduce the noise level.

How loud is loud? Here is a simple guide:

- *Do you have to shout to be heard 2 metres away from someone?*
- *Are people's ears ringing after leaving the workplace?*

If noise levels are unacceptable you must carry out a noise assessment. This should identify the workers affected and their daily noise exposure, and identify control measures. You should be aiming to reduce the noise level at source or contain it in some way, for instance by enclosing the activity that is causing the problem. You should only provide staff with hearing protection *(see page 42)* as a short-term measure or as a last resort if all other efforts at reducing the noise level have failed.

The HSE *(www.hse.gov.uk)* provides further information about the legal requirements relating to noise and a guide for employees on how to protect their hearing (*'Protect your hearing or lose it!'*).

Slips, trips and falls

Common accidents
The most common kind of accidents and their likely causes are:

- *slips caused by wet floors, unsuitable footwear or loose floor coverings*
- *trips caused by obstructions in walkways, trailing cables or uneven floor surfaces*
- *falls caused by unstable ladders or unsafe guard rails.*

**Caution
Wet floors**

What can you do to help prevent these common accidents?
Practise these simple housekeeping measures:

- *Mop up spilled liquids straight away and use signs to indicate when floors are wet.*
- *Ensure that there are no trailing cables across walkways.*
- *Keep the workplace clear of obstructions and build-up of waste materials.*
- *Ensure that people have enough light to see where they are going.*
- *Improve visibility and add floor markings if there are changes of level or slopes.*
- *Ensure employees' footwear is adequate.*
- *Display warning signs or put up barriers to protect your staff and customers when there is a potential hazard.*
- *Encourage staff to be aware of potential hazards and to look out for signs of circumstances that might lead to an accident taking place.*
- *Carry out risk assessments (see page 12) to identify the types of hazard present on your premises, and take appropriate measures to control them.*

The HSE provides further information and leaflets about accidents; see their website *(www.hse.gov.uk)*.

Electricity

What are the main hazards associated with electricity?
- *Contact with live parts – the electrical injury may also be compounded if the shock causes the casualty to fall from a height, such as from a ladder.*
- *Faults that could cause fires.*
- *Fire or explosion where electricity is the source of ignition.*

Is your electrical equipment safe to use?

Whatever you use, take appropriate steps to ensure that the equipment is safe to use and does not put the operators in danger. With portable electrical appliances – those that can be plugged into the mains supply – you must arrange for them to be tested for electrical integrity (PAT testing) regularly. The frequency of these tests will depend on your assessment of the hazard and risk posed by the equipment. If you are in any doubt about what you need to do, you should call in a qualified electrician to advise you.

Controlling the risks
Help to control the risks by:

- *selecting the right appliance for the job*
- *making sure that the electrical installation is safe, e.g. don't overload sockets*
- *reducing the voltage where possible, for instance by using battery-operated power tools rather than mains-operated ones*
- *ensuring that installations include appropriate safety devices, such as fuses, residual current devices or circuit breakers*
- *not allowing any work to be carried out on electrical appliances by unqualified or unauthorised persons*
- *arranging for testing of the integrity of your mains supply at least every five years*
- *arranging for testing of the integrity (including earthing, insulation and fuse rating) of all portable electrical appliances at regular intervals*
- *checking plugs and cables regularly for signs of damage or wear and tear, and replacing them as necessary*
- *arranging regular maintenance of machinery by suitably qualified persons*
- *taking into account the conditions in which electricity is used – e.g. out-of-doors, in wet surroundings – and taking appropriate precautions*
- *taking faulty equipment out of use immediately*
- *switching off appliances before plugging in, unplugging, cleaning or making adjustments.*

Hand–arm vibration

It may be a hazard for your staff to use hand-operated power tools such as drills and hedge trimmers for long periods or frequently. Types of problems that may result include:

- *vascular disorders – symptoms are tingling and numbness in the fingers*
- *neurological disorders*
- *bone and joint disorders*
- *muscle disorders*
- *other problems including headaches, fatigue and sleeplessness.*

Hand–arm vibration syndrome

The HSE proposes that employees be asked the following questions to see if they have any symptoms of this disorder:

- *Have your fingers gone white on exposure to cold?*
- *Have you had any tingling or numbness after using vibrating equipment?*
- *Have you experienced problems with the muscles or joints in your hands or arms?*
- *Do you have difficulty picking up small objects?*

If your business involves use of hand-operated power tools, carry out a risk assessment *(see page 12)* and implement appropriate controls, such as:

- *buying the lowest vibration equipment possible*
- *issuing thick gloves to absorb at least some of the vibration*
- *padding the handles of the tools to do the same*
- *limiting the exposure to the hazard by ensuring that staff take frequent rest breaks or change periodically to different tasks that do not involve using this equipment.*

Chemical hazards

Do you use substances that give off fumes or vapours, or cause irritation (e.g. solvents or cleaning fluids)? Be aware of the conditions under which they should (and, more importantly, should not) be used – refer to the Control of Substances Hazardous to Health Regulations 2002 (COSHH).

Do you know what to do if someone spills, inhales or has physical contact with such substances? Manufacturers and suppliers must provide this information by means of material safety data sheets, which should accompany the goods. Staff should have suitable and sufficient information before they start to use the substances.

Risk assessment
Assess and implement appropriate control measures. Ideally, find a way to avoid the need for the substance(s) to be used at all, or try to find alternative (less harmful) products. If it is not possible to replace them, ensure that all sensible precautions are taken to avoid any ill effects from using them.

Is there frequent exposure to chemical hazards?
If exposure to hazardous substances is more constant than irregular, use a consultant to carry out COSHH assessments.

Are you selling potentially hazardous products?
If you sell potentially hazardous products you must provide your customers with safety information. General guidance is usually shown on the container: 'Irritant' or 'In event of contact with eyes...', and this should be sufficient for most items sold over the counter.

Hazardous substances

Problems caused by hazardous substances and how to deal with them

Some people are allergic to dust, vapours, gases and other hazardous substances *(see also chemical hazards on page 61)* and suffer from allergic reactions such as asthma or skin infections if they are exposed to them.

Under the Control of Substances Hazardous to Health Regulations 2002 (COSHH), employers must control exposure to hazardous substances to protect the health of their staff. Ideally, if staff are affected by hazardous substances you should move them to different jobs where they will not be exposed to the hazard that causes the reaction. If the job cannot be changed, you must try to keep the employee separate from the hazard, ensure that she or he is exposed to the substance for as little time as possible, and provide appropriate personal protective equipment *(see page 42)*.

Biological hazards

If your business involves dealing with blood or other body fluids you should ensure that your staff are adequately protected from contact with these substances (such as the provision of disposable gloves and aprons), and that the fluids themselves, any soiled materials and any implements used in the work (especially 'sharps') are disposed of as special waste *(see page 66)*.

If you work with animals, be aware that there are diseases you can catch from them. Implement appropriate controls to minimise the risk of infection.

Risk assessment

If any of these circumstances apply to you, carry out a risk assessment *(see page 12)* of activities that might be hazardous and identify any additional control measures you can take to reduce the risk of contamination or allergic reaction. Consider engaging the help of a qualified consultant as this is a specialised area of risk management.

Asbestos

Almost all ill health and deaths related to asbestos today are the result of exposure that may have occurred decades earlier, when asbestos was commonly used for insulation and lagging in buildings during the 1950s to the mid-1980s.

Legal obligations

You have a legal obligation under the Control of Asbestos at Work Regulations 2002 (CAWR) to:

- *take reasonable steps to find any asbestos-containing materials on your premises*
- *assess the condition of any such materials found*
- *ensure that any materials found are safely sealed and labelled*
- *prevent exposure of employees to asbestos, or that exposure be controlled to the lowest possible level*
- *know what to do – and who to contact – if the asbestos is likely to be disturbed*
- *maintain a log and plan of the location and condition of the asbestos-containing materials.*

If your work involves building repair and maintenance, or if you are having alterations made to your premises, you should ensure that a survey has been carried out by a qualified contractor before the work commences. Employees, or any contractors working on the premises, must be informed if a building contains asbestos, and the location of the asbestos.

You can find out more about asbestos from the Health and Safety Executive (HSE) or the Control of Asbestos at Work Regulations 2002.

Vehicles

Is there any risk of an accident taking place on your premises that is caused by a vehicle? If so, you should do all you can to minimise this possibility. The following are some of the measures which could reduce the chance of an accident caused by a vehicle taking place:

- *Change the layout of the area where vehicles operate.*
- *Prevent vehicles reversing by introducing one-way routes.*
- *Segregate vehicles and pedestrians by marking routes clearly.*
- *Display warning signs (see page 43) for drivers and pedestrians.*
- *Introduce speed limits and making sure they are observed.*
- *Install speed humps or other physical measures to prevent drivers driving too fast on site.*
- *Ensure that any workplace vehicles are maintained and inspected regularly, and that they show and sound warning signals when reversing.*
- *Ensure that drivers of workplace transport are suitably trained and have up-to-date licences.*
- *Loading and unloading procedures for vehicles such as forklift trucks, cages, rubbish lorries should be carefully considered, and a risk assessment (see page 12) carried out.*

If an accident occurs you must record it in your accident book and investigate it as appropriate *(see page 52)*.

10 Environmental issues

The following are environmental and waste issues that you, as a business must consider, be aware of, and carry out where applicable.

Pollution prevention

All businesses need to take care about what goes down their drains (e.g. no waste oil or chemicals). All domestic sewage must be discharged to a foul sewer for transfer to the sewage works. Surface water drains (e.g. in the gutter) must only be used for clear water, as the discharge is not treated before it goes into rivers or soakaways. For further information about the correct storage and disposal of wastewaters and other liquids, contact your local council, the Environment Agency, or the Environment and Energy Helpline (freephone 0800 585794).

Climate change levy

This tax on energy use was introduced in April 2001 and is added automatically to your energy bill. Look at your most recent bill to see how much you were charged in the period for the levy. Typically, it adds round 10% to the cost of energy. The aim is to encourage businesses to reduce the amount of energy used in the UK and help the UK reach its target of reducing the amount of carbon dioxide (the global warming gas) produced to 20% of the 1990 levels by 2010.

Duty of care

Under waste law, you must store your waste properly and prevent it from harming the environment. You must also ensure that all waste collected from your store (including any recycled waste) is transferred to an 'authorised person' such as the council or a waste contractor. Whoever collects your waste must have a licence to carry waste and should give you a document known as a waste transfer note that describes the waste and its origin. Under the law, you must keep all waste transfer notes for at least two years.

Landfill tax

In 1999, the Government imposed a tax on all waste sent to landfill. This tax is designed to penalise the excessive use of landfills and to encourage businesses to reduce and recycle waste. This tax is one of the reasons why the cost of trade waste collections has gone up and is continuing to increase. The tax is currently £13/tonne of waste, but will increase by £1/tonne every year until 2004. However, as the Government is under pressure to bring the landfill tax in the UK into line with the rest of Europe, this could see the rate doubling to £26/tonne. Implementing the requirements of the EU landfill directive in the UK will also result in increased landfill charges – which will be passed on to you.

Packaging waste regulations

These will apply to stores, as a seller/retailer, to recover and recycle a certain percentage of their packaging waste. The regulations currently apply to companies with an annual turnover of more than £2 million and which handle more than 50tonnes/year of obligated packaging. Re-used packaging is not classed as obligated packaging. To find out more about the regulations and how to calculate packaging waste obligations, contact the Environment and Energy Helpline on 0800 585794.

Hazardous waste

The Environment Agency regulates the disposal of hazardous waste (special waste). A consignment note must accompany every movement of hazardous waste. Everyone involved with the transfer of hazardous waste must retain a copy of the consignment note. In addition, copies must be passed to the Agency. The Environment Agency website gives you more details *(www.environment-agency.gov.uk)*.

11 Legislation

The following statutes and regulations are those most likely to be relevant to your business but there are many more that are industry specific:

Consumer Protection Act 1987
Data Protection Act 1998
Disability Discrimination Act 1995
Employers' Liability (Compulsory Insurance) Act 1969
Employers' Liability (Defective Equipment) Act 1969
Employment Act 2002
Environmental Protection Act 1990
Fire Precautions Act 1971
Health and Safety at Work Act 1974
Occupiers' Liability Act 1984
Sale and Supply of Goods Act 1994
Sunday Trading Act 1994
Supply of Goods and Services Act 1982
Trade Descriptions Act 1968

Control of Asbestos at Work Regulations 2002
Control of Substances Hazardous to Health Regulations 2002 (COSHH)
Electricity at Work Regulations 1989
Fire Precautions (Workplace) Regulations 1997 (as amended 1999)
General Product Safety Regulations 1994
Health and Safety (Consultation with Employees) Regulations 1996
Health and Safety (Display Screen Equipment) Regulations 1992
Health and Safety (First Aid) Regulations 1981
Health and Safety (Miscellaneous Amendments) Regulations 2002
Health and Safety (Safety Signs and Signals) Regulations 1996
Health and Safety Information for Employees Regulations 1989
Lifting Operations and Lifting Equipment Regulations 1998 (LOLER)
Management of Health and Safety at Work Regulations 1999 (MHSW)
Manual Handling Operations Regulations 1992
Noise at Work Regulations 1989
Packaging (Essential Requirements) Regulations 1998
Personal Protective Equipment at Work Regulations 1992
Price Marking Order 1999

Producer Responsibility Obligations (Packaging Waste) Regulations 1997

Provision and Use of Work Equipment Regulations 1998 (PUWER)

Reporting of Injuries, Diseases and Dangerous Occurrences Regulations 1995 (RIDDOR)

Safety Representatives and Safety Committees Regulations 1977

Sale and Supply of Goods to Consumers Regulations 2002

The Special Waste Regulations 1996

Working Time Regulations 1998

Working Time (Amendment) Regulations 2002

Workplace (Health, Safety and Welfare) Regulations 1992

Copies of the above may be obtained from The Stationery Office Ltd or downloaded from *www.hmso.gov.uk*.

12 Useful sources of information

There are a number of places from which you can obtain further information on any aspect of your business where you find you need more help. These include:

ACAS Helpline (for employment law) – *www.acas.org.uk*

British Retail Consortium – *www.brc.org.uk*

British Safety Council (for publications and training courses) – *www.britishsafetycouncil.co.uk*

Business Link – *www.businesslink.org*

Disability Rights Commission, helpline: 08457 622633 – *www.drc-gb.org*

Environment Agency – *www.environment-agency.gov.uk*

Food Standards Agency – *www.foodstandards.gov.uk*

Health and Safety Executive (for HSE publications and website), HSE Infoline, confidential telephone helpline: 0870 154 5500 – *www.hse.gov.uk*

HMSO (for text of legislation) – *www.hmso.gov.uk*

Information Commissioner's Office, information line: 01625 545745; notification helpline: 01625 545740 – *www.dataprotection.gov.uk*

Local authorities (Environmental Health and Trading Standards departments) – *www.tradingstandards.gov.uk*

Microsoft bCentral (advice for small businesses) – *www.bcentral.co.uk*

Trade associations

Index

ACAS (Advisory, Conciliation and Arbitration Service) 31, 69
access
    disabled 37
    public and visitor 44–5
accident books 52
accident prevention 51, 58
accidents 45, 51–2, 58
Acts of Parliament 67–8
age-related sales 21–2
alcohol
    age-related sales 21
    Sunday trading 24
asbestos 63

'best before' dates 26
biological hazards 62

calibration of equipment 16, 19
CCTV (closed circuit television) 23
chemical hazards 61
cleanliness 26
climate change levy 65
clothing
    see protective clothing and equipment
communicating with staff 36
computer games, sale or renting of 22
computers 23, 47
consignment notes 66
consumer rights 11, 20
contractors' safety 45
Control of Asbestos at Work Regulations (CAWR) 2002 63
COSHH (Control of Substances Hazardous to Health) Regulations 2002 61, 62

danger signs
    see signs and notices
data protection 23
disabilities 37
Disability Discrimination Act (DDA) 1995 37
disabled access 37
disciplinary procedures
    by enforcement officers 10

staff	32
discrimination	32, 37
electrical equipment	59
emergency procedures	8, 36, 51
employees' rights	31–8
employers' liability	
certificates	8
insurance	15
employment law	31–8
Sunday trading	24
energy use tax	
see climate change levy	
enforcement officers	9–10
Environmental Health Office (EHO)	9–10
environmental issues	65–6
equal opportunities	32, 33, 37
equipment maintenance	41, 56
eye tests	47
failure to comply penalties	10
fire	53–6
signs and notices	8, 43, 54–5
fire alarm testing	54
fire drills	54
fire extinguishers	55–6
inspection and servicing	56
fire marshals	54
fireworks, sale of	21
first aid	51
first-aid signs	8
first-aiders	51
flexible working	34
food	19, 25–6
Food Safety Act 1990	25
Food Standards Agency (FSA)	25
fork-lift trucks	41
goods and services regulations	18–20
age-related laws	21–22
grievance procedures, employers and employees	32

HACCP (Hazard Analysis Critical Control Points)   25
hand-arm vibration syndrome   60
    see also RSI (Repetitive Strain Injury)
hand-operated power tools   60
hazardous substances
    biological and chemical   61–2
    waste materials   66
hazards   14, 44, 57–64
health and safety   8, 11
Health and Safety Executive (HSE)   9, 45, 52, 69
hearing damage
    see work-induced hearing loss
hearing impaired disability   37
holidays, staff   35
hours of work   24, 34

imperial measures   19
improvement notices   10
information, sources of   69
Information Commissioner, The   23
injuries to staff   40, 47, 57, 60
insurance   15

labelling, food and goods   19
landfill tax   65–6
landlords' responsibilities   14
learning disability   37
legionnaires' disease   50
legislation   67–8
licences   17
lifting operations   41
lighter refills, sale of   21
lone workers
    see working alone
lottery tickets, sale of   21

maintenance of equipment   41, 56
Management of Health and Safety at Work Regulations 1999   12
management responsibilities   7
mandatory signs
    see signs and notices, mandatory signs

manual handling	40
maternity leave and pay	33
see also paternity leave; pregnancy, and working; new mothers	
metric measures	19
National Insurance contributions	33
National Minimum Wage	33
new mothers	46
noise	27, 57
non-compliance penalties	10
non-refundable goods	20
occupational sick pay	33
Occupiers' Liability Acts 1957 and 1984	14
outdoor working	48
overtime	34
part-time staff	32
PAT testing (electrical equipment)	59
paternity leave	33
pay	32, 33
permits-to-work	45
physical disability	
see access, disabled; disabilities	
pollution	65
pregnancy, and working	46
premises regulations	14, 44
pricing goods	19
product liability insurance	15
professional indemnity insurance	15
prohibition notices	10
proof of purchase	20
protective clothing and equipment	26, 42, 48, 57, 62
public liability insurance	15
public safety	44–5, 52
racial discrimination	32
record keeping	12, 13, 16, 52
redundancy	35
refunds	20

regulations
  see *Acts of Parliament*
Reporting of Injuries, Diseases and Dangerous Occurrences
Regulations (RIDDOR) 1995   29, 52
risk assessments   12
  electrical equipment   59
  fire   53
  hazardous substances   61–3
  manual handling   40
  new and expectant mothers   46
  vehicles   64
  working alone   49
  young people   38
road warning signs
  see *signs and notices, road warning signs*
RSI (Repetitive Strain Injury)   40, 47
  see also *hand-arm vibration syndrome*

safety information, chemicals   61
safety requirements, sales of goods   18
salaries and wages   32, 33
second-hand goods, labelling of   19
'sell-by' dates   26
sewage   65
sex discrimination   32
shared premises   44
short-term contract staff   32
signs and notices
  age-related   21–2
  fire   43, 54, 55
  hazard signs   14, 44
  mandatory signs   8, 43
  road warning signs   64
  safety signs   42, 43
  warning signs   43
solvents, sale of   21
staff injuries   40, 47, 57, 60
staff training   13, 35
  fire   56
  first aid   51
  food hygiene   26
statutory sick pay (SSP)   33

stress	30
Sunday trading	24
tenancy agreements	14
terms and conditions of employment	34
Tiger (Tailored Interactive Guidance on Employment Rights)	31
tobacco, sale of	21
Trade Descriptions Act 1968	18
Trading Standards	17
uniforms	
see protective clothing and equipment	
VDUs	47
vehicles, safety in workplace	64
videos and DVDs, sale or renting of	22
violence against staff	29
visitors' safety	14, 44
wages	32, 33
warning signs	
see signs and notices, warning signs	
waste	65–6
waste transfer notes	65
water	50
weights and measures	19
work equipment	39, 41, 47
work-induced hearing loss	57
work-related upper limb disorder (WRULD)	
see RSI (Repetitive Strain Injury)	
working alone	49
working conditions	27–50
outdoors	48
Working Time (Amendment) Regulations 2002	38
Working Time Regulations 1998	34, 35, 38
Workplace (Health, Safety and Welfare) Regulations 1992	27–8
workplace safety	13, 39, 57
workwear	
see protective clothing and equipment	
young people	38